Cultivating
PURPOSE

LIKE A SEED LET YOUR PURPOSE UNFOLD
STEP BY STEP, STAGE BY STAGE

ESTHER SINCLAIR

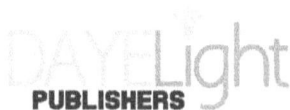

DAYELight
PUBLISHERS

ISBN: 978-1-949343-60-1

Acknowledgments

I dedicate this book to the Holy Spirit, who gave me the inspiration, and to my wonderful family, including my church family and friends. You have been a great source of support and strength during this journey.

To my immediate family, my wonderful husband, Dillion, and four beautiful daughters: Samantha, Danielle, Jada and Ruthanne, you have taught me so much and you truly are the wind beneath my wings. I could not have done it without you.

To my extended family, especially my mom, Rebecca Hayle, who is a tower of strength and to my four siblings: Christopher, Joylyn, Keisha and Steve, you are my rock.

Love you all!

Table of Contents

Acknowledgments iii

Introduction 9

Stage 1: (Genesis Stage)

Acknowledge the 'Acorn' within You 13

    The Mystery of The Seed 18

    What's the Big Deal about a little Seed? 19

Stage 2: (Genesis Stage)

Break up that Barren Ground 25

    The Standard for the Soil 30

    What's the Point of the Process? 32

    The Process of Brokenness 33

Stage 3: (Germination Stage)

Cultivate under the right Condition 41

    The Strategy of the Sower 45

    What's the Chance of Maximizing Your Capacity? 47

    Take A Chance: Make A Change 49

Stage 4: (Germination Stage)

Discover that which is Dormant 57

The Rhythm of Times and Seasons 62

What's the Use of Rushing through Life's Cycle? 64

Stick to Life Rhythms or get Stuck in Life Seasons 66

Stage 5: (Growth Stage)

Emerge Once Your Roots Are Established 73

The Dimension of your Systems and Structures 78

What's the True Measure of your Resilience? 80

Challenge Every System That Threatens Your Stability .83

Stage 6: (Growth Stage)

Flourish and be Fruitful 89

The Connection to the Source 94

What is the Driving Force of Your Productivity? 96

Reproduce by Multiplying your Impact 98

Stage 7: (Growth Stage)

Grow into your Greatness 105

The Subjectivity of the State of Nature 110

What is the Shift Required to change your life's
Trajectory? 112

Get out of your Comfort Zone: Get on a Growth Trajectory 114

Success versus Greatness 116

Conclusion 121

Introduction

Don't attempt to read this book, unless you have prepared your mind to embrace truth. Jesus stated in St. John 8:31-32 that if we continue in His word, we are His disciples and we shall know the truth, and the truth shall make you free. For we know in part and we prophesy in part. But when that which is perfect is come, then that which is in part shall be done away. (1 Corinthians 13:9).

On my journey to the path of purpose, I realized that my way only became clearer after I had an encounter with the Spirit of truth, who guided me deeper into God's truth. I always knew I wanted to teach, but not in the regular classroom setting. As I delved into the Bible, the Word of truth, it became the vehicle to get me to my destination. That was when I fully grasp the mystery of purpose, which is not trying to understand it as a whole but embracing its unfolding. This led me to look at the pattern and principles of the seed, and the lessons it reveals about purpose.

When you tell God: "I want the truth more than anything else," He will reveal His truth to you in a variety of ways, such as, through creation, your conscience and also through careful consideration. Truth is knowable. You can test it, experiment with it and prove it because all truth are parallel, so in order to understand a spiritual truth, we can look at the natural example of it. Nature encompasses everything that falls under the laws of physics, and these truths are practically applied in this book.

Seeds are kingdom principles. They represent one of the most powerful elements in nature and its concepts are applicable, both in the natural and spiritual realm. The Bible applies natural truth by using farming images, especially in parables, to reveal deep spiritual truths, which are applicable in our everyday lives. Those who seek to excel in God's universe, must have regard for these divine principles. God's wisdom is revealed to us in all of creation.

Planting seeds and getting harvests are an essential part of God's design, as well as being an essential part of His nature and character. It is a fact that the seed, when understood correctly, can greatly improve people's lives, and it is my prayer that the trajectory of your life will shift to another level and you will be inspired to greatness as you read this book.

Stage 1
(Genesis Stage)

Acknowledge the 'Acorn' within You

You are frustrated because you keep waiting for the blooming of flowers, but you have yet to plant the seed.

~ Steve Maraboli

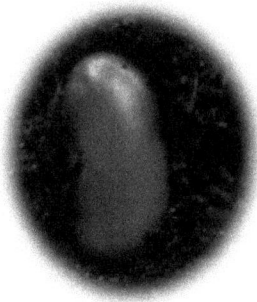

"People say I have a great calling on my life (mixed feeling), but idk (I don't know). I do want to get what God has for me, but sometimes I don't see what ppl (people) tell me is inside of me. I DONT KNOW WHERE TO START! It's really hard!"

~ Youth mentee

L et's face it, life can feel quite complicated at times, especially during the turning points or transitional periods of your journey. You will agree that sometimes it can be puzzling when your mind, like a continuous maze, is constantly bombarded by the myriads of unanswered questions, especially the "why am I here" and "*what should I do*" questions. Perhaps you are already caught up in this maze as you search frantically, hoping to find the answers to propel you towards what you consider to be the right path, yet the same questions continue to baffle you, making you feel confused and overwhelmed, not knowing which path to take.

SO WHERE DO WE START?

First, we must see ourselves from God's vantage point - He knows our end before He declares our beginning *(See Isaiah 46:10).* Whereas right now we are still trying to connect the dots, He promised to guide us every step of the way. Knowing His plans to prosper us *(See Jeremiah 29:11)* and His heart towards us will help us have the confidence to step into our truest identity. There we are affirmed, realigned and that is the place where all those mystifying moments will be resolved once and for all. As you embark on this journey, don't make the mistake of always setting your face to the future without recognizing where you are in the present moment. We are guilty of spending too much energy trying to figure out *"our end"* or our destination *and we have not even* begun the journey. If you are unsure about where you are heading, now is the perfect time to start. The beginning of this journey is only a small step, but don't despise small beginnings *(See Zechariah 4:10)* because it will enable you to appreciate very early how your purpose as a whole unfolds *"step by step* and *stage by stage."* When we learn to see the pursuit of our ultimate purpose as a journey, and NOT a destination, then we will embrace each moment as cherished opportunities.

You don't have to be great to start, but you have to start to be great.

~ Joe Sabah

Like the seed, we can appreciate that everything 'BIG' usually starts with something small. A tree starts out small, and eventually blooms into something big, once the conditions are favorable. It is important for us to establish this foundational truth early, which illustrates to us *the necessity of beginning,* especially as we start this journey. In fact, the very foundation of everything seen and unseen is simply this: "*Everything has a beginning, it all begins with a seed!*" Likewise, everything that exists in this world was once an idea: a seed-thought which was first conceived and then nurtured over time to come into fruition. Big businesses or ventures were birth out of small ideas or hobbies which someone was willing to act upon. When you understand that God releases His blessings to you in seed form (See Genesis 8:22), then you will allow that seed to attach itself to the core of your being so that it will begin to fill that space where vision and purpose comes alive.

Did You Ever Think About This?

You began with a seed: What you eat began with a seed. The roof over your head, the clothes you WEAR; fundamentally, everything begins with a SEED.

The Mystery of The Seed

"Man is wise and is constantly in quest of more wisdom; but the ultimate wisdom, which deals with beginnings, remains locked up in a seed."

~ Hal Borland

God's divine order is established in the Earth by a system of laws and principles that govern the entire universe. The plant lifecycle starts with a seed, and this God-inspired reproductive system enables us, His creation, to fill the Earth and, therefore, become self-sustainable. This foundational concept of the seed is sealed by the first law that God established in the Earth: the *law of seedtime and harvest,* as recorded in the book of Genesis: *the book of beginnings.* Just in case *you overlook it, this law is in operation 24/7 and is intended to last* for as long as the Earth remains, to govern everything; *seen and unseen (See Genesis 1:11).*

"How does this relate to me?" you might ask, the mystery is: you are not empty. There is a seed that God has placed deep within you when you were created, and that seed contains your DNA; the secret formulae for your success. In the parable of the mustard seed, Jesus taught that even though this seed is so small and insignificant when it is planted, it produces a great tree with great purpose *(See Matthew 13)*. Now you know you have been empowered at creation with the ability to reproduce the seed within, the intensity of your relationship with God is key to unlocking the secret formulae in your seed because there can be no conception without intimacy. Understanding this mystery can help you tap into the manifest wisdom of God, the Creator, and get a revelation of His plans for your life, as you apply the many truths locked up in the seed.

> See a Flame in a Spark; a Tree in a Seed. See GREAT things in little Beginnings.
>
> ~ Richard Sibbes

What's the *Big Deal* about a little Seed?

The power within the seed, so small, yet such greatness is hidden on the inside. It is called potential; the power within the seed.

God created everything on Earth with potential. Potential energy is a term used in Physics for unused energy or stored up energy. It is dormant ability, reserved power, untapped strength, hidden talents or capped capability. *Wow! Think about that for a minute; that is energy that has not yet taken action.* It is all you can be, but have not yet become, and the endless possibilities of what you can do, but have not yet done. If we don't utilise our potential energy to fulfil our purpose, we will never feel fulfilled.

Everyone came into this world fully loaded with potential, designed to enable them to achieve all they can dream of achieving in life. The strength of the oak tree is very present in the acorn, although not yet manifested. Imagine that acorn seed; as small as it is, it has an enormous amount of stored energy woven deep within its DNA to create a huge oak tree. If something as small as an acorn seed can fulfil its purpose by using energy to create something so beautiful, powerful, and life-sustaining, imagine what we could do with our potential energy.

'Everyone is born with Potential, yet few people really understand what it is, and fewer realize that discovering their full potential allows them to change their fate, redefine their destiny and, ultimately, change their world'.

Believing is Key to Beginning

We are all packed with potential. We just have to look within to find it. Your ideas and intuition are all God-given seeds, a recurring pattern or a defining moment that connects us to "our self." What we believe about our seed is key. The problem is not with our make-up or where we were born, neither is it with our family, whether they are poor or rich. The problem is in you discovering the gifts and abilities deposited in you at creation and doing something about it. Once we accept that greatness is already planted deep within us, our journey has begun. If we allow our feelings or other people's opinions to dictate whether we have significance or not, we will end up feeling incomplete.

Now is the time for us to apply this knowledge so we can fully tap into the unexplored potential which lies within us. As we embark on this journey, let us allow the 'acorn' within us to grow and be transformed into the towering oak it was created to be. Accepting and believing are keys in the starting process because we might not even feel as if we are great but know this: *Greatness is not a feeling, it is a pursuit.*

Every seed is a seed of destiny, because it has the capacity to influence your future.

Every seed is a seed of significance, because it has the potential to make a difference.

Every seed is a seed of promise, because it promises to bring about a bountiful harvest.

Summary - Acknowledge the Acorn within you

Dig Deeper

TRUTH See the pursuit of purpose as a journey, not a destination. To start, you must begin with the understanding that God made everyone with potential and it is your duty to acknowledge it and activate it.

For Further Research

- Potential energy versus kinetic energy.
- Seed concept based on creation from the Bible.
- The journey of the acorn seed to the oak tree.

Related Topics

- Understanding your desires and design.
- Your S.H.A.P.E (Rick Warren).
- Your personality.

Stage 2
(Genesis Stage)

$\mathscr{B}$reak up that $\mathscr{B}$arren Ground

You can't plant seed without first breaking ground.

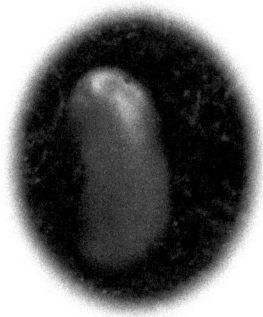

"Why, God, Why? Why does bad things happen to good people? Why must I go through this!!

~confused youth

So you have acknowledged your God-given potential and feel all charged up and ready to fulfil your God-inspired dream - wow - feels great, right? The truth is, that great feeling is just the start of your story, to provide the momentum to keep you moving forward, but that is just the beginning. There are other details usually lost in the fine print, which are necessary to prepare you for the middle aspect of your journey, once you decide to stick around.

Here we accept that the path which takes us to the promise is not always a smooth or straight one, but is intercepted with thickets and thorns, and delays and detours. Storms will come, relationships will be tested, and your fears will be confronted. You might find yourself asking the question: "Is this journey still worth it?" The answer is a resounding yes, but only to the extent that you are teachable and willing to completely surrender your will and accept the reality that ultimately you are <u>NOT</u> the one in control.

Why Do I Have To Go Through This?

We ask why because we don't understand the unfolding of the big picture concerning our lives, but God knows. He is omniscient *(all-knowing)* – (See *Psalms 147:5)* - and has a standard set for each one of us, which must be met before we can advance to the next level. God's plan may sometimes lead us through a difficult path because He is intent on 'extracting from us that which the enemy would love to use against us.' When we try to figure everything out, we become anxious and overwhelmed, thereby, giving the enemy access to rob us of our peace.

When we accept His leading, instead of fighting against it, detouring from it or just outrightly going in the opposite direction, we become less anxious. *'When we can't trace His hand, we can trust His heart' these words from a popular song* is the standard of submission to His divine process taken from a popular song. Now is the time to slow down and trust because each of us are on a different path, which is so unique, that only God knows the details. As it unfolds, be determined to stay the course and trust God, even when you can't see what lies ahead.

> God has a master plan or a blueprint concerning our lives, which must be worked out in His time and according to His standard. At this stage, He is more interested in what He can do IN YOU than what He can do THROUGH YOU.

It is a fact that the seed cannot be planted, unless the ground is first broken up. Although it can be quite painful and messy, this is a precondition for sowing and is the most effective for the soil to receive the seed. This *"first things first"* concept gives us a glimpse into the mind of God, the Creator, and helps us understand why He is so intentional and accurate. He knows that there are things within us that we are unaware of, and if that is not dealt with in a timely manner, it could greatly hinder the development of our seed. Therefore, He is patiently waiting to work a good work within us, to prepare us for what He has prepared for us. That is why He **designs everything we go through to fulfil a specific purpose**. No matter how you try, you cannot shortchange God's plan. There is no quick fix or shortcuts, so you might as well stay the course. Like the soil, why not just surrender to what

God determines is most effective for you to prepare you for your ultimate purpose.

> *Know this: God does nothing on impulse. Every hair on our head is numbered. Everything on Earth has its proper time and seasons. Every experience is designed by God to fulfil a purpose.*

The Standard for the Soil

Purpose begins with the seed, but **growth depends on the soil.**

Good ground is not automatic; it requires great effort. All farmers know that the quality of the harvest is not dependent only on the seed, but on the condition of the soil. Therefore, preparing the soil is critical and, perhaps, the most important step in the entire gardening process. In the first parable: the sower and the seed *(See Matthew 13)*, Jesus taught that although there were four different soils, only the good soil had the capacity to produce the abundant harvest. The word "good" in the Greek is *kalos*, which denotes: "that which is well adapted to its circumstances." This suggests that it has the potential for exponential growth because it has less obstacles and more room for the seed to thrive.

30

Like the soil, God must first do a work in us, which requires getting rid of anything which could possibly impede or obstruct His divine purposes in our lives. In His wisdom, He understands that until key elements are removed from the soil of our hearts, it makes no sense to plant the seed of greatness in it. We all want to be used by God, but any soil destined for Him to use must first meet the "good soil" standard, that is, it must be receptive and adaptive. You don't have to be a garden guru to understand the significance of planting in soil that has been loosened up. So, create good ground for your crops by replacing fear, doubt and negativity with positive truth and this is achieved at a place called "surrender"; when we become open to God's process, that is, whatever method He has designed or series of actions that He has taken in order to achieve a desired result or to accomplish a specific goal or purpose in us, for our good and for His glory. Wow! That is truth!

> **Learn to appreciate the process, though you may not celebrate "the PROCESS." You may not even embrace or enjoy "the process," but if you want to accomplish God's will for your life, you MUST go through the PROCESS.**

What's the *Point* of the Process?

When God wants to make a giant oak, he takes 100 years, but when He wants to make a mushroom, He does it overnight, *because greatness depends on process, and process takes time.*

It is a requirement that before any architect designs a building, they first ask the question: "What will be its purpose? How will it be used?" This knowledge will be incorporated in the buildings blueprint to guarantee that it can stand up to what it was designed for. This concept known as "**form follows function**" (*3-F rule)* is the pervading law in architecture, which guides all design decisions and it also determines the time, resources and strength-tests the building will have to endure, to prepare it for the required use.

God, who is the Master Architect of our lives, designs every process we go through to achieve His specific purpose. He determines what *"form"* our lives will take, to prepare us to fulfill our *"function"* (*3-P rule: Promise + Process = Purpose).* You are not built to break, so if He has prepared a calling for you, then He must prepare you for your calling. This was the pattern for the Patriarch, Joseph, who was called and given a promise, after which came his process: *"Until the time that his word came: the word of the LORD tried him." (Psalm 105:19).*

Preparation is one facet of living in order. When you are prepared, you are attentive and ready for action. You honor your boundaries and make yourself available, when you are prepared. Preparation helps you avoid living wastefully and squandering your time and resources. Understanding this truth will help you embrace your various preparation processes, because once you are called, prepare yourself for the coming season of training and preparation. *"Preparation time"* is never *"lost time",* so the greater your "purpose," the greater will be your "process" because on this journey, *"process"* must precede *"purpose."*

The Process of Brokenness

"It takes broken soil to plant seed; broken clouds to give rain; broken grains to make bread." ~ Vance Havner

Broken soil is fertile soil. Like the breaking of ground, being broken stirs up greatness within us. We sometimes question the path our life might have taken, especially if we have been battered or abused, and we wonder why a loving God would allow this to happen to us. However, if we truly believe that: "All things work together for *(our)* good" *(Romans 8:28),* then we can appreciate that *"all things"* includes everything that will impact our lives to prepare us for our purpose. Know this: "Fruit is always birthed out of the soil of our soul and its broken places." You can't come into the fullness of God, unless you come through brokenness. There is no getting around that reality. Even the best of us need to be broken, because without process, there is no progress.

> *"We are fertile ground, broken by troubles, enriched by failures and watered by tears."*
>
> *~ TD Jakes*

Who Wants Anything Broken?

God does! He uses broken things. We are cultured not to appreciate broken things but, through God's eyes, brokenness is something we should desire, not a condition to be fixed, because it is what opens us up to His grace. It is a fact that some of the most fertile lands were built by volcanoes, which effectively got the toxins out of the soil. Life does that: it presents challenges that forces you to: "turn and till the soil" and dig deeper to find a way to work through or around the obstacles in your way.

The process of brokenness, as depicted through the soil, is one ideal illustration of how God wants to accomplish His divine purpose in and through us. Once the soil is broken up, the real work begins. The roots you don't want, along with the rocks, pests, and any hard lumps of soil, must also be removed. *Sounds like fun, doesn't it?*

Genetically modified dreams will produce genetically modified results, so while you are anxious to see the end results, never attempt to forego the process.

What Must Be Broken?

Our hardened hearts, as a result of sin and pride, must be broken. Our selfish and stubborn wills must be shattered, so the will of God will be at the center of everything we do. Our heart is the birthplace of our destiny. Like the soil, it is the place where the seed of greatness finds a place to sprout. Left to itself, it is not considered fertile but desperately wicked and barren *(See Jeremiah 17)*. Barren land, as we know it, is unproductive and hard to penetrate, so it requires the most effective tool, like a plough, to dig deep and bring those things below the surface up to the air and light.

God's word, sharp and powerful, is the best tool to till the soil of our hearts, softening it and breaking clods of resistance, which keep the seed of God's word from penetrating and taking root: *designed to make us receptive and responsive.*

When our heart is receptive to the word of truth, it is likened to ground which is continuously being ploughed.

Brokenness is God's requirement for maximum usefulness because hidden in some of those big disappointments, are treasures of truth that literally transform our lives and our future. Through adversity, failure, and disappointment, He molds us into people whom He can use.

We are, each of us, in our own way, broken soil turned over and over by all types of circumstances in our everyday lives. However, we will soon find that:

This brokenness, which we often so desperately try to hide;
This brokenness, that we think disqualifies us from God's love;
This brokenness is the very thing that allows the seed, the Word, <u>God's love to take root in us</u>."

~ Nancy Leigh DeMoss

Dig Deeper

Summary: Break up that Barren Soil

TRUTH Your response to the various experiences, testing and trials you go through on your journey, will determine if you reach your destination. The seed of greatness already planted in you, needs good ground, in order to produce the hundredfold. So work continuously on your heart ground.

For Further Research

- Different processes on our journey.
- What more can we learn about brokenness.
- The heart ground.
- Parables about the different soils.
- Importance of the principle preparation.
- Building code: forms follow function rule.

Related Topics

- Understanding how unforgiveness and bitterness affects your journey.
- Complete surrender of the will.

- Delays and detours: your response, and what it teaches you about your journey.

Stage 3
(Germination Stage)

Cultivate under the right Condition

The seed that makes great, is not the seed that lies fallow, untrained and unattended to. Rather, it is one that is properly cultivated, nurtured, pruned and garnished under the right atmosphere and conditions.

"I have big dreams, but, perhaps, hopefully, maybe one day I will get there."

~ Youth mentee

L ife is what you make it. If you believe this truth, then don't just drift through life; live intentionally and on purpose. Make your life count by finding the time to stop and take stock of it. An attitude of intentionality gives you permission to live decisively. Ask yourself this question: "Am I seizing the opportunities that come my way or am I just sitting on the fence living by default?" Your response will determine the actions you take from this point onwards. Like a game of chance, the outcome is dependent on your next move, which will either cause you to advance forward or wander in the wilderness of regret. Right now, you may not know the what, when or how of your journey, but don't delay because, chances are, you will never know until you take that next step. For those of us who are willing to intentionally navigate their way, by God's grace, the end result will speak for itself.

What's The Next Step?

If you want to achieve anything in this life, it will be as a result of aggressive action and intention. Truth be told, the future does not belong to the dreamer, it belongs to the doer. Once you pay attention to the key indicators in your life, such as, your gifts and passion, you will be fully prepared to seize that perfect opportunity, as your gift makes room for you. Otherwise, you will just be selling yourself short. When you make up your mind to step out by faith, and trust your spiritual instincts to guide you, you will live on purpose by executing action and diligence, which will empower you to arrive at a place called destiny. So, don't delay; it is decision time. Start cultivating because your future depends on it.

> *Every morning you have two choices: continue to sleep with your dreams or wake up and chase them.*

Broken ground, although such a powerful process, is absolutely meaningless without planting seeds. Purposeful planting is the most strategic action that the sower must execute, if he intends to reap a bountiful harvest. It is a fact that our present location, people who intercept our lives (our destiny helpers), our level of preparation and abilities are all critical components that will create the right opportunity for the seed of greatness planted within us to prosper. Therefore, when a seed lands in your heart, whether it is a vision or dream, you must be deliberate about feeding and nurturing it. This seed must be cultivated in the best environment and continuously watered to create enough capacity for it to grow and flourish without hindrance. Until this is accomplished, the seed remains in a dormant state, with unrealized potential.

Knowing this truth should propel you to take action by making it your ultimate responsibility to ensure that every seed entrusted in your care is passionately cultivated, until it blossoms into a fruit.

> *The potential within you is a seed that you must passionately cultivate until it becomes a fruit.*

The Strategy of the Sower

Cultivation is the EFFORT a farmer makes to bring his garden to its full capacity.

The sower understands that the work of farming does not end with planting the seed but starts with cultivating it. If he does not make the effort to be active every day in his garden, tending to his crops, even the best seed will remain unproductive, even though unlimited creative potential lies within it.

The first responsibility that God gave Adam was to *"tend and keep"* or *"cultivate and guard"* the Garden of Eden *(See Genesis 2:15).* This required of him to **make it his priority** to have a vision for his garden, to bring it to its full capacity by investing time to nurture each seed from conception until birth. The productivity of the garden is his responsibility to execute, and once this potential is activated, the forces of nature will complete the process.

> *"The price of greatness is responsibility."*
>
> ~ *Winston Churchill*

We are the gardeners of our lives. Once we observe this principle, life becomes one of order and fruitfulness, but if we are lazy and fail to cultivate, nature will follow its course and our garden will degenerate. In the parable of the ten talents (See Matthew 25:14-30), the lesson is taught that you can choose to invest your seed by making great

46

effort to cultivate it or neglect it by making excuses; either way, there is a great price to pay, so it pays to have the right strategy. When we make it our priority to fully explore who we really are, we engage ourselves in progressively unlocking our sense of purpose, which maximizes our capacity and is essential to our happiness and longevity. The responsibility is, therefore, placed squarely on us to make the sacrifice to cultivate the greatness which is already planted within us.

Ever wonder why, despite the fact that we all have the seeds of greatness within us, we don't plant them or nurture them, to reap the harvest of greatness?

What's the *Chance* of Maximizing Your Capacity?

*Unless you **pay the price** for success, you will never know its true worth.*

If you want to fulfill your destiny, you must make a choice to take the chance to seize every opportunity that comes your way, or your life will never change for the better. Think about your life as an investment and if you should apply the investment concept to

47

your life for a moment, and start by measuring the value of opportunities realized, lost or wasted, just how much would be your possible net worth? Although this type of assessment is usually applicable when considering investment opportunities, it also measures the opportunity cost: the value of lost opportunities and the benefit of the thing you could have done, instead of what you are doing now. When we refuse to take action, the opportunity costs of our decisions are most expensive because opportunities realized are only attainable to those willing to pay the price.

Expand your capacity for greatness by diligently exploring all the possibilities that lies within you.

Like every seed, we have a built-in divine code of instruction called our DNA, which equips us with the ability to grow and develop our true capacity. This is the sum total of all the resources God has placed within us. We are God's investment and He knows our true worth, so we must be deliberate about developing our gifting and enlarging our capacity. The truth is, the price tag we put on ourselves will determine what we get back in return, so when we envision our life as an investment, this type of focus will propel us to take advantage of all the opportunities available to us. So, seek to become a person of value by investing in yourself. Take action and seize available opportunities, rather than seeking success[1] because "capacity never lacks opportunity", as it is sought by too many anxious to use it.[2]

> **Destiny is where purpose meets opportunity at the right time and place.**

Take A Chance: Make A Change

Some people succeed because they are destined to, but MOST people succeed because they are determined to.

Every day contains countless opportunities to take action that will affect our future. Most times the difficulties we experience in life open doors that allow each of us to make that shift to do what we really love. There is that great opportunity of acting on a new idea, a new plan or writing a book, but the challenge in making that decision requires us

---

[1] *Albert Einstein*
[2] *Bourke Cockran*

to do something different from what we are doing now: make a change.

Why is it that some people are so productive, while others continue to squander their lives away? It is because they have the audacity to act. Change is not failure. It is okay to change; change your mind, change your environment, change your situation. Embracing change means embracing life, which gives us the capacity to grow and create. Although it comes at a cost, it determines whether we *"grow and survive"* or *"decay and die."*

Change Your Choices, Change Your Chances

Your true worth can only be realized in the right environment because genes do not act out of their environment, but in relationship with it. Be prepared to change your internal and external environment, until it is conducive to the germination of your seed. This is the kind of change that will challenge mindsets and force you to take action. Too often we unconsciously put ourselves in environments that are an obvious misfit to our gifts and abilities, then we question our level of success.

God designed us with intuition, and other signals of discomfort, to indicate to us the necessity for change. This is set up on purpose to propel us to the right place, out of our comfort zone and it empowers us to realize our true worth. If you feel like you are undervalued, like how a fish feels out of water, perhaps it is time for a change. Don't ignore the warning signs; that is why fishes can't be what they are created to be out of water. It is time you seek to find an environment where your genius is valued and cultivate it within that environment and to the right audience. The change required might just be the push you need into a bigger and better ocean.

> *"The price of inaction is far greater than the cost of making a mistake."*
>
> *~ Meister Eckhart*

Inaction has a cost; it is the cost of not growing, of not being remarkable, of not being the very best you can ever be. Most people want to live their best lives but refuse to take action, until the pain of their current condition exceeds their fear of change. So, challenge yourself and refuse to allow inaction to rob you of your destiny. Take a chance on yourself, get started on living your dreams by taking one small step in a new direction. When you do, you will take full advantage of the opportunities available to you, and this effort will unleash the infinite possibilities for greatness in your life. Otherwise, you are just selling yourself short.

Action is the key to success and action is what separates the successful from the unsuccessful. If you have the courage to say yes to the direction your life should be heading, you will be amazed at how the pieces will come together for you. Stop waiting on someone to confirm what you already know in your heart, because no external force, however powerful or influential, can awaken your potential for you. It is your duty to take deliberate efforts to explore it for yourself, because **the more focused you are on something, and take action connected to it, the more doors will open, and the more life will give you a chance to get closer to your vision.** It is the price you must be willing to pay, because some moments you cannot get back, some seasons you cannot relive, and some doors will never be opened to you again. Too bad only a few choose to embrace these endless possibilities.

"Happiness is not something you postpone for the future. It is something you design for the present."

~ Jim Rohn

Dig Deeper

Summary: Cultivate under the right Conditions

TRUTH The success you want to achieve will be as a result of aggressive action and intention. It will not fall into your lap you must have the audacity to act.

For Further Research

- Explore the price of inaction.
- Capacity building in every area of your life.
- Embracing change.
- Importance of the environment you cultivate yourself in.
- Lessons from Scripture about the different stewardship.
- Importance of the principle of responsibility.
- Measuring opportunity cost for your life.

Related Topics

- Investment principles for life.
- Living an intentional life.
- Having a strategic life plan and goal setting.

- Living without regret.

Stage 4
(Germination Stage)

Discover that which is Dormant

The perfect unfolding of a seed's potential is determined at each stage of its growth.

"I'm always getting great prophesies about what I'm capable of, but nobody notices me!"

We want results, and we want them now! So, you have been sowing and watering your seed but still not seeing the immediate results. You have been asking God "When?" and, quite frankly, you feel stuck because you are waiting too long, while others around you seem to have gotten the green light. Even though it is quite normal to feel frustrated or make comparisons, the reality is, it won't change a thing! Although we exist in this new "instant" world, we must not be fooled into thinking that everything is instant. We have unconsciously conformed to the new *"microwave generation",* thinking that *faster* is always better, and this mindset often carries over into us always rushing to the next big thing.

At this stage, the principle of patience is a must because you are powerless to control your growth process. Truth is, it is pointless to rush, because there is a specific blueprint for your life, which must be followed, and that design has a specific timeline, which will unfold in perfect time.

How Long will It Take?

Our attempts to speed things along and do things in our own way and in our own time, will only distort the process. If we choose to follow the course of nature set for us, then we will respect the time needed for growth and maturity and, depending on what our mission is in life, our time will definitely vary. Although we may believe the problem is "when", the real issue is making sure we are prepared when our appointed time shows up.

Once we understand that our story is still unfolding, we won't feel stuck in life because **we will allow ourselves to gradually become who we were meant to be, instead of adapting to the role we are expected to play.** However, most of us miss this truth, and we see this very often in people who change jobs every year, and even spouses in pursuit of greener pastures. This is not the time to be anxious and make permanent decisions based on temporary circumstances, so stay put and wait for your season of manifestation.

> *There is no magic wand to take us instantly to where we need to go. While you believe in miracles; never believe in shortcuts.*

Any successful gardener who wants to achieve exponential growth must first seek to acknowledge the pattern automatically in place to facilitate growth. Germination is a fundamental law of growth and everything in nature follows this pattern. It is easy for us to state the "why" and "what" we want to achieve in life, but the "when" and the "how" is totally beyond human jurisdiction. The soil only provides a platform for the seed, which is already preprogrammed to manifest in its own time, as the seed can lie dormant for years, until the conditions become favorable to facilitate its growth.

Only God, in His wisdom, knows the specific time and season for each seed that has been sown to germinate. That is why we have laws: natural patterns, time cycles and seasons, which are in place *on purpose* to provide the perfect opportunity for every seed to grow. So, even though right now it may appear dormant, just trust His timing and nature's pattern because it is never too late for a seed to germinate.

> *Seeds don't sprout until it is the right time. Some of our efforts - the seeds we plant in our lives - don't always grow when we want, but when the time is right, things will take off.*

The Rhythm of Times and Seasons

Opportunities are tied to the seasons of a man's life, designed and created to move him to the next level.

When God created the Earth, He divided the elements into times and seasons, which represents the order of nature. This pattern is established through the main cycles: the annual seasons and the 24-hour cycle of time. As a result, all of nature moves in rhythm as it cycles through times and seasons effortlessly and naturally. These cycles serve as an instrument of measurement and assessment to execute God's plans.

In the parable of the growing seed (See Mark 4:26-29), Jesus tells of a farmer who scattered his seed and trust it to the forces of nature, while he went about his business day by day. The seed sprouted effortlessly, and he did not know how. This illustrates that the experienced farmer understands that if he doesn't act in harmony with nature's pattern, he will miss his harvest.

To everything there is a season, and a time for every purpose. (See Ecclesiastes 3:1).

Our lives also move in cyclical rhythms, just as in nature. An understanding of the cycles of life will help you to trust its forces to guide you and take advantage of the opportunities available to usher you to the next level. Every cycle is designed to facilitate our growth, which is never an instant process because life is full of structure and trajectory, and some seasons are simply designed to cultivate momentum for what is to come.

So, if you aim to live in the rhythm of God's seasons for your life, then you must use these experiences to ask yourself: "What can I learn?" and "How can I grow?" This is the opportune time to shape, structure and develop your vision, until it is ready to manifest, because it can be very dangerous to give you what you are not matured to receive.

Life is built in seasons. Miss it and you will lose your harvest.

What's the *Use* of Rushing through Life's Cycle?

"Nature does not hurry, yet everything is accomplished."

Your destiny is like an unborn child going through the various developmental processes, but when it reaches full maturity, there is a birthing process. This period of maturation, also known as the *"gestation period"*, represents that timespan between conception and birth or over a period of time when an idea or vision takes form. All creation has a gestation period (or lifecycle), which controls the "when" and the "how" of the growth process and determines our readiness for the next level. It is not always subject to specific timelines, like a natural pregnancy but, like the process of germination, it is dependent on the type of seed. Different seeds have different needs; therefore, this season cannot be rushed.

The key, therefore, is to be patient, like the farmer, who acknowledges that he cannot force the results. He appreciates that the potential within the seed is not something to rush to get, but something to turn within and unlock, and this process involves a time of waiting and a time of patience.

Each seed is unique and failure to acknowledge the germination period of different seeds will result in the sower terminating or sabotaging the growth process by continually exposing the seed to one's anxiety and impatience.

Through the seed's entire growth cycle, it grows, step by step: first the blade, then the ear, then the full grain in the ear *(See Mark 4:28)*. The universe is created in perfect harmony to facilitate your transition in-between life seasons. The seed cannot miss or skip steps but must stick to God's order or rhythm for its growth or risk producing premature fruits.

It is very easy to get excited about the big picture but not wait for the where, when, and how of your cycle. Whenever we are tempted to rush God, He reminds us that, like the seed, we also have our own cycle, which involves time, and He works through that process. Many times, we are tempted to try and speed it up by skipping stages we may consider as irrelevant to us, only to find out the hard way when our lesson must be repeated. Once we respect the process of growth and wait on our gestation period by accepting each circumstance that God has sovereignly placed us in as part of our process, we will see the results, and the less anxious we will be.

Scientists have proven that a seed can lie dormant for years, but given good soil and water, it will germinate and do what it is preprogrammed to do. So, resist the urge to be anxious and abort the seed chances by digging it up to see if it is sprouting, because you will only render it useless.

> **Be careful not to shorten the life of your dream by trying to short-circuit the natural progressions set out in the seed.**

Stick to Life Rhythms or get Stuck in Life Seasons

Be very careful not to postpone your plans
and ideas because you are frustrated with
time and get stuck in the season of delay.

You can transition naturally and effortlessly through the cycles of life, once you understand that they are temporary. Those of us on a journey of growth go in and out of seasons, and we need to honor each season on our journey and the journey of others. The season of dormancy is designed to deepen our knowledge of God's soveignty as He builds our character, while we wait and surrender to His control.

One of the most difficult lessons we must learn is how to wait the right way, otherwise, we become frustrated with the process. We must wait in a way that makes us a participant in what God is doing, and not someone who struggles against the wait. Embracing the wait, while applying some key principles such as delayed gratification, which is postponing immediate reward until later, is key to your maturity. It is not our natural inclination to wait, but we all benefit from the wisdom gained in the waiting room because that is where we are transformed into who we are destined to become.

Although it will threaten the intensity of our vision, stretch and strip us until we are ready to sprout, this transitional period: period of "hidden-ness"; "preparatory phase", "wilderness time", or whatever it is called when no one notices you, holds a purpose. It is designed to test your real motive and mature you; but not to destroy you.

The problem with waiting is not having all the details, especially when the time between sowing and reaping feels like eternity, and the place between God's answers feel like a desert where dreams and faith go to die.

God has a specific place and time for the vision, dream or idea He has given you, and it needs time to grow and mature, before you see the results. If you want to be in sync with His will, then you must learn how to discern the proper times and seasons.

The ancient Greeks had two words for time: Chronos and Kairos. The former refers to chronological time, while the latter refers to proper or opportune time. "Kairos Season" is God's perfect timing, as He brings the right people, at the right place, to accomplish His will for your life. Knowing this should equip you to understand your seasons so you will know when you are faced with an opportunity or a life trap. It is time to live in your Kairos moment and not put off what should be done right now or sit around waiting for the perfect moment when all is safe and sound to act. It makes no sense either to hold on to seasons long after the expiry date has passed, wishing you could live your life over again.

> *"Waiting is not about what I get at the end of the wait, but who I become as I wait."*
>
> ~ *Paul Tripp*

Perhaps your vision has been shelved because you believe time has passed and your seed is now dead but know this: your God-given seed cannot decay; it is incorruptible; it is still alive and still metabolizing. Now is the time to carry it to full-term and not allow doubt, fear, insecurity or naysayers to cause you to abort the vision God has placed in your heart. There is greatness in you, and it is time to manifest the genius within. Now is the time to get ready; it is not time to give up, but to live with expectation and discover what has been lying dormant all this time because God is getting ready to transition you from hidden to highlighted!

> *"The greatest tragedy is when a tree dies in a seed."*
>
> ~ *Myles Munroe*

Dig Deeper

Summary: Discover What Is Dormant

TRUTH   God has designed the universe with seasons and cycles, and our lives follow a similar pattern. Therefore, you should patiently wait on your cycle to be completed, and not try to rush it. If you rush it, you could possibly abort it.

For Further Research

- Explore the principle of patience.
- Understanding proper times and seasons (Kairos season).
- Embracing the period of hiddenness, until you are highlighted.
- Importance of learning the right way to wait.
- Lessons from Scripture about the work of patience.
- Transitioning from being stuck to sticking with your rhythm.

Related Topics

- Dealing with anxiety issues.
- Stages of maturity and sonship.

71

Stage 5
(Growth Stage)

Emerge Once Your Roots Are Established

Taking an out-of-sight, out-of-mind approach to your roots, will only result in weak roots and an unhealthy plant.

"I see everybody stepping out and doing their thing and I believe now is my time!"

There is something special about a purpose whose time has come. The vocation for your life is starting to peak above the ground and it is exciting. This is really a moment to celebrate, because after a long period of sowing and laboring in the fields, the signs of harvest are finally here.

When the surface is broken, we finally begin to see what we have been working towards, and we rejoice because we stayed the course and did not throw in the towel. It is now time to break forth. Sounds great, right? But are you ready to emerge? Are your systems and structures firmly grounded? Is your foundation stormproof? Well, if you are not sure, trials and tribulations have a way of showing up the cracks in your surface. At this stage, the focus is not so much on what is happening above ground, as exciting as that may be, but the necessity of a firm and solid structure below.

Who Am I Beneath the Surface?

It is a fact that before you establish anything in life, you must first seek to build a strong foundation that will hold the structure in place. Establishing an unshakable foundation is key to your stability and gives you a firm footing from which you can emerge. If your foundation is not solid, then you won't have the strength to emerge or forge ahead into new territories. Understanding your true identity, and what drives you, is key to your stability, because if you cannot clearly define who you are, then you give others permission to define you on their own terms.

What you know about how you are wired gives you a foundation on which you can build. It encompasses what you believe with all your heart, your convictions about life and your character and value system. Do not make the mistake to neglect these unseen things because that is what keeps you grounded and brings stability to your life. So, dig deep and nurture that which supports and help you determine where your boundary lines fall.

> **The deeper you believe in who you are, and what you stand for, the deeper your roots plant themselves firmly in your foundation.**

When a seed's cycle of maturity has ended, it is usually time for it to emerge, but not before confidently answering these questions: "What are the chances of its survival? How strong are its roots?"

God designs different seasons to give us structure and stability because He knows that without roots, we are nothing. Many people believe that attending every seminar and reading every self-help book is the key to being ready, but the root of the issue is the issue of the roots. Unless you have a strong support system, you are at risk of not remaining viable after you emerge.

Our God-given destiny also needs strong and deep roots to keep it anchored, and sustain it so that when it grows, it can withstand the harsh winds of life. Now we understand why many dreams have sprung up prematurely and die an untimely death, because the inner qualities of character and motives were not given roots deep enough to strengthen it and wide enough to establish it during the difficult times. When onlookers see our tree, they only see the visible; how successful and big the tree is, but they don't see the invisible; how deep and wide our roots are, and how they bend underground as they overcome the obstacles of life. This is at the heart of our foundation and it is what gives our tree its resilience.

> *"A tree is more than its fruit. We must cultivate our whole selves from the roots up."*
>
> *~ Thomas Merton*

The Dimension of your Systems and Structures

A Tree with strong roots laughs at the storm We must understand the correlation between how deep and firmly planted the roots are, and how strong the tree is!

Nearly everything we know about plants is from the ground up. We don't usually see the roots, but we see the results: a strong healthy plant and its fruit. It is critical, however, to know what happening beneath the surface.

A strong root system must keep pace with the size and dimension of the tree it supports, by adjusting its structure in response to the environmental conditions, in order to weather life's storms. So, the bigger the tree, the more resilient the roots need to be, so it won't succumb under pressure. The roots must grow deep, like a tap root, to anchor the plant in the soil and grow wide, like a fibrous root, to draw nutrients from every available source. The parable of the wise man who built his house on a rock, illustrates to us this principle that a solid foundation is required to keep your house anchored to withstand the storms (See Matthew 7:24-25).

> **The world we live in is both complex and interconnected; to survive, we need a multi-dimensional approach to our personal growth.**

The plants root system is a reflection of our support system. It should grow deep in the form of self-development, and grow wide by connecting with systems and people, which supports the achievement of our goals. When we take proactive initiatives to strengthen our foundation, we develop the resilience to adapt and keep pace in this ever-changing world.

You are the blueprint portrayal of your foundation, so strengthen those roots and equip yourself with the power of habit, by investing in support systems that keep you sturdy and expands your horizon. Most importantly, remain true to yourself by nurturing your value system because, whereas other systems may change over time, values have deeper roots and longer life spans.

> *You are interested in how fast you grow, but God is interested in how strong you grow.*

What's the *True Measure* of your Resilience?

Pressure can strengthen what you already have or blow up and expose the weaknesses you struggle with.

It is the depth of your conviction, the breadth of your interests and the height of your ideals that will determine whether you bend or break under pressure. Though it is easy to deceive many people while in the shallow, pressure is a true reflection of who you really are in the deep. The relationship between pressure and depth is best illustrated under water, and it suggests that the deeper you go, the greater the pressure. At sea level, you don't feel much pressure, because the fluids in your body are pushing outward with the same force, but as you go deeper, the forces of gravity are greater and, therefore, challenges your level of buoyancy.

So, to be truly resilient, you must understand how to operate from a place of depth. The iceberg model best reflects this principle, as it is easy to underestimate the size of the iceberg for some ships because the bulk of it is invisible to the eyes, but that is where the power to face pressure is derived: from what is submerged. This emphasizes to us the danger of functioning or seeing people from a limited dimension or at surface level. When people see us, they make an assessment based on face value, but they must know there is a greater part hidden beneath and this is what determines our level of impact and reveals our true stability.

Iceberg Hidden Logic: **the invisible lays the foundation for the visible. Ships that ignore this ice "below the water" are in mortal danger.**

A proactive approach to strengthening our roots of resilience is a necessity for successful living. Trees need wind-pressure as they grow, to strengthen their root systems in order to be able to withstand the heavier winds when they are in full bloom.

Resilience must be developed ahead of time, before you face a major crisis. This is work that is done under the surface, behind the scenes, and this largely unseen work doesn't get much attention or applause. No one notices weak roots, until the tree has died but by then, it is too late. If you think you can build strength of character during your trials and hardships, you are gravely mistaken, because hardship doesn't build character; it just reveals it.

Nature illustrated this process quite beautifully through the Chinese bamboo tree, which for the first four years spends most of its energy on root development in preparation for its explosive growth in the fifth year. This is a lesson for leaders, especially, who should make sure their root system grows with them in order to be effective. The health and growth of these systems are maintained by continuously turning the spotlight within.

Many people look like mighty trees, but when you cut below the surface, their roots are almost nonexistent. Learn to appreciate your grind by working twice as hard on your character and value system because character, more than competency, is your main support system to keep you rooted and grounded.

> *"True character is revealed in the choices a human being makes under pressure: the greater the pressure, the deeper the revelation, the truer the choice to the character's essential nature."*
>
> *~ Robert McKee*

Challenge Every System That Threatens Your Stability

At the root of every matter, is a root cause.

Studies have shown that an estimated eighty percent of plant problems start underground, hidden from the human eye. Everything has an underlying structure; some are physical, such as, bridges or buildings, and some are nonphysical, such as, the plot of a novel or the form of a symphony. Altogether, these serve a great purpose, as both represent your foundation: the invisible layers of your life that cannot be ignored. The structures in your life help you to stay focused and effective, whereas the systems are the processes and routines that equip you with the power of habit to support the achievement of your goals.

Most of the issues we face involves us building our lives on a faulty foundation, which leads to self-sabotaging habits that are difficult to uproot. The truth is, the power of any system lies in the fact that what we do habitually, we become permanently. Right now, you should be thinking about addressing all those areas of your life that threaten your stability.

Your <u>foundation</u> is key! The rest is just a chain reaction.

It takes more than willpower to be determined to let go of the damaging habits that have become ingrained in our subconscious, taking us along a fixed path. Renewing our thinking through a process of transformation is the only change we can make that will threaten that system (See Romans 12:1-2). We can start by applying the principles of displacement and replacement, which is to examine different aspects of our lives, including our relationships, with the intention to recognize and correct unproductive patterns and, if needs be, to walk away from deeply rooted beliefs and behaviors that doesn't support or add value to who we envision ourselves becoming. This will help us to realign our thinking and strengthen our support systems, like our inner circles, with the values and attitudes that best represents who we really are.

Transformation doesn't happen in isolation; it needs a plan and a support system.

We cannot remain in darkness and isolation forever. Like a butterfly, when the time comes to be pushed from our cocoon, we must be prepared to emerge. Although we may not be able to see it, the years of struggle and pain were very effective in producing something underground, which has taken root and shape. We understood ourselves better in the face of pressure, and the values which keeps us anchored.

For the truly resilient person, adversity is not the only prerequisite to advancing towards your goals. Although our life experiences have taught us well, some of the most valuable lessons we can learn are from the stories of others. We should seek to study those who are successful in their fields and have walked similar paths like us, with the aim to gain wisdom as we pursue our goals. When we get a glimpse of what our goal looks like, as it breaks through the ground, our responsibility is to keep strengthening those roots, despite the difficulties, and keep moving forward, as we fortify our resilience to continuously grow and evolve.

> *"Only a fool learns from his own mistakes. The wise man learns from the mistakes of others."*
>
> *~ Otto von Bismarck*

Dig Deeper

Summary: Emerge Once Your Roots Are Established

TRUTH There is a set time for everything, and once your vision reaches full maturity, it is time to emerge. However, if you did not fully prepare yourself, your roots will succumb to pressure, and you will fail. So, it makes sense to do the work underground first.

For Further Research

- Evaluate your response in the face of pressure.
- Understand which systems are faulty and could destabilize you.
- Embracing and strengthening the support system you have in place.
- Importance of being proactive by preparing for the storms of life.
- Lessons from Scripture about the strong foundation.
- Practicing to function from a place of depth.
- Applying the iceberg principle to your life.

Related Topics

- Understanding your EQ (Emotional Intelligence), and not just your IQ.
- Investing in your character, and not just your competency.
- Operating in wisdom and learning from the mistakes of others.

Stage 6
(Growth Stage)

Flourish and be Fruitful

God does not just bless us to be strong shade trees, but rather flourishing fruit trees.

"I have worked hard and paid my dues. IT'S ALL ABOUT ME living it up now!"

At the beginning of our journey, our main goal was about our quest to connect the dots to our purpose and achieve success, but as we make progress and gain more understanding and dimension, our main concern now is all about the extent of our impact. Before, we may have felt incompetent, undervalued and unfulfilled, but now we realize that the vision for our lives is much bigger than us, and this realization has given us permission to make our mark in a world where darkness is disguised as light.

The world is indeed waiting to receive all the good fruits our lives were designed to produce. Therefore, we will not feel fulfilled until we have made a deposit that will change the world for the better. This confidence gives us the energy that will drive us to be the change we want to see.

What Difference Can I Make?

Is the world a better place because you are here? Nothing that is of significant value can be achieved, unless we first have that sincere desire to make a difference. The positive deposits we make today, creates the opportunity for us to flourish and produce a harvest of greatness tomorrow. There are many points of view, which equates flourishing with becoming more mindful, instead of being more fruitful. It is the good we produce, however, that unlocks our destiny, empowering us to make our mark and create even a little spark that will illuminate our corner of the world.

We have so much to offer the world but, unfortunately, our own beliefs, thought patterns and fears can squash that truth and make us forget. Despite these obstacles, however, we must fuel our drive to go after what appeals to us, rather than leaving them on the dusty shelves of our cluttered minds. At this stage, the focus should be to find our compelling "why", to give us a clear sense of purpose connecting us to something greater within. Once we find that spark, it is our duty to pursue it, and gradually fine-tune what it represents.

"You playing small doesn't serve the world. As you let your own light shine, you indirectly give others permission to do the same."
~ Marianne Williamson

Our deep roots have given us the power to grow beautiful fruits, and we have a mandate from our Creator to multiply and be fruitful. Everything we need to flourish is already placed "in" us, as the fruit we bear gives us a taste of eternity. Whatsoever our lives were designed to produce, defines our eternal impact as humans, which is unique to us because different trees produce different kind of fruits. What is interesting about this fruit is that it is not only for us to enjoy, but for others to partake of and, if it is not utilized, it falls to the ground rotten and useless. A fruitless tree is a poor testimony, although it may be a strong shade tree, because it has failed to recreate itself. When we reproduce the seed that has been planted within us, we feel fulfilled because we have a clear sense of purpose and, therefore, qualify to leave a legacy. None of us desires to live a useless life, so once you understand what your purpose on Earth is, share it with the world, and don't get caught up with storing it up for yourself.

> *Fruits are known to have a lasting impact. The seed bears a fruit and the fruit, in turn, bears seeds, which then bears more fruit, ad infinitum.*

The Connection to the Source

"The power of purpose is as potent as the energy of focused light when connected to its source."

In order to produce fruits, our seeds of greatness must first connect with the light of promise for new life to begin. Light is important for life and no living thing cannot function without a central source to sustain it. Think about how the seed must push itself through so much dirt, until it finds the light of the sun. Once it finds that light, it gets a new platform for growth and a new level of life begins.

The seed's source of sustenance is the sun, and if that fails to light up, all lifeforms it sustains would die. Thankfully, the sun in the sky gives light to all lifeforms, so every seed that finds this light, finds life. Now we know why the first declaration God made at creation was: "Let there be light" *(See Genesis 1:3),* because He is light and He understands that without this positive force, nothing on Earth can be sustained.

A candle loses nothing by lighting another candle.

~ James Keller

We cannot connect to our light, without connecting to our source. Once we make that connection, the same energy that gives life to everything around us, will activate the light buried deep in our souls. This light represents what illuminates our path and drives us. When we focus this light like a laser beam or a spotlight, it becomes even more powerful. As we live a life that is in alignment with who we really are, we ignite the light within by connecting to our ultimate purpose. The power of this focused energy will help us to shine so brightly that we can equip others to find their switch, and that is when we become unstoppable and relentless.

Many people lose their focus and feel disconnected because they believe they do not have the right platform to make a difference. The truth is, however, no matter what the situation, you have the power to choose your focus by finding the light to drive you or by being that light in the midst of the darkness. When you learn to create a spark wherever you are, it propels you towards your goal because it is in finding our light that we are most productive and become a conduit of illumination.

It is during our darkest moments that we must focus to *see the light,* because it is never too late to find our heart and get it out in the open.

What's the *Driving Force* of Your Productivity?

If you have a positive driving force that is compelling you forward, you are unlikely to wear out, slow down or give up.

What drives your life? What compels you to get up and go in the morning? It is called passion, and it is the driving force for all successful winners, movers and shakers of this world. A study was commissioned in a specific manufacturing industry, and workers were told they were participating in a study on productivity. Little did they know that the only change in the environment was brightening the lights a tiny bit and, as a result, productivity soared. Even when the lights were dimmed again, productivity continued to climb, because light energizes and what you focus on, and where light shines, it grows. Every living thing, including people, needs light to shine on them to be productive.

This positive energy that sits inside of us is the light within that is unlocked whenever it connects to purpose. It goes beyond motivation and will truly energize you on a whole different level. So, endeavor to find this light and, once you find it, refuse to remain in darkness, and resist the temptation to enjoy it all by yourself.

> **Focus on what you are genuinely passionate about and let that guide you to your destination.**

You can't grow plants by giving them light once or twice a month, and the same goes for people. We will never feel fulfilled, until we connect fully to something we are passionate about. This connection will cause us to tap into our mental reserves, as our heart becomes ignited to fulfil a specific desire by focusing on that one thing we can do better than everyone else. When that is absent, we end up feeling unfulfilled, frustrated or just going through the motions.

Most people embark on a path of anguished soul searching for their passion, which leads them to purchasing numerous self-help books, and attending many seminars, but still they can't find the answer.

Embedded in that pursuit is an erroneous belief that passion, when seen, will be immediately recognized. The truth of the matter is, when we follow what lights up our brains by exposing our heart to what we love, in the same way that the plant leaves open up to the sun, that energy will drive our actions and lead us to the right destination. We are all searching for meaning or a state of being, and when we discover our 'sweet spot' or our 'ikigai' (*a Japanese concept for our reason for being)*, that is where we are most productive. Once we function from this place, we are able to maximise our sense of meaning, and multiply our impact.

Reproduce by Multiplying your Impact

*The true prosperity of the tree comes when
the tree produces fruit for others to enjoy,
and for the reproduction of more trees.*

The reproductive stage is the final stage of the growth cycle, and that represents the stage where the plant flourishes, as it uses its energy to beautify its environment and multiply by producing seeds. It is only when we lose our seed by sowing it in the lives of others can it multiply and reproduce, and our impact will outlast us.

We may teach what we know, but we reproduce who we are.

The term flourishing, although a Biblical concept, is very popular today because it fits very comfortably into this new individualistic, secular culture with its self-centered and unsustainable focus. When we understand that we have a duty to sustain life by multiplying our God-given seeds, we realize it is not solely about us but about what we leave behind, which is our legacy. Our legacy is the positive impact you can have, which is locked up inside of you. Whatever you discern your mission to be, think of the legacy you want to leave, because our greatest purpose, as humans, is to mature and grow in order to leave a legacy that outlives us.

Deep down, embedded in everyone's heart, is the desire to leave a legacy and impact more people than they could have done on their own. We don't have to wait until we die; we can live that legacy every day. For some people, this is the driving force, leading to great and extraordinary contributions to humankind.

Those whose main goal is to make money seldom make an impact, as their focus is on attaining success, while significance and legacy is lacking. Can you imagine if the power of multiplication takes over, as we lose our seed in the lives of others by equipping the next generation? Although it goes against our selfish ambitions and pride, the returns are worth the investment.

> **Don't live for the temporary; live for the fruit that lasts.**

The platform of leadership gives us a great opportunity to have impact through the power of multiplication as we serve. At its heart, it is more about influence than position, more about being a force for the positive. We might not always see the fruits of our labor, but If we want to accomplish something great, something that lasts, we will eventually see the impact we have, to remind us of the power we have to make a difference.

Great leaders are like lighthouses when they use their light to guide others on the right path. It encompasses investing your time into doing what you were born to do and shining bright so that others can see their way. If you are a solo act or the kind of leader who doesn't share the stage or the credit with others, you will not have this impact. When we spend time to openly recognize the contribution of others, we give them permission to shine, and make them feel valued and special. Now you can unlock a lighthouse of possibilities, by encouraging others around you to find their light and make a positive difference, and that is all it takes to change the world.

"Lighthouses don't go running all over an island looking for boats to save; they just stand there shining."

~ Anne Lamot

Summary: Flourish and Be Fruitful

TRUTH Once we connect to God, our main source, we will ignite our passion and that will enable us to be productive. We are created to be fruitful and to multiply, but the fruit we produce is not just for ourselves; we must see the bigger picture. When we have that mindset, we are destined to leave a legacy.

For Further Research

- Explore your passion. What lights you up?
- Understand the impact of positive forces and positive energy to propel us forward.
- Understanding the power of multiplication.
- Importance of being your authentic self and reflecting your light.
- Lessons from Scripture about legacy and impact.
- Practicing productivity by being a force for the positive.

- Use whatever platform you have to be productive.

Related Topics

- Understanding that passion is explored, based on your everyday actions.
- Research 'IKIGAI' and function from different quadrants in your life.
- Mentor and train, but you must have impact and reproduce.

Stage 7
(Growth Stage)

Grow into your Greatness

Great people are not born great; they grow into their greatness.

*"I am a totally different person NOW than I
was before starting this journey."*

L ife happens in Cycles of Seven this stage
may signal the end of a cycle of growth;
now our journey takes on deeper meaning
as we journey to greatness. Greatness is not
by chance, neither is it the elusive concept that we
believe it to be. Rather, it is a choice that we make
every morning when we get up. Our life is like a
puzzle, and every day we should be open to discover
another little piece, because there is more to our
story than the picture we have developed in our
mind.

Once we accept that growth is an ongoing process,
we are on the right path to discovering more about
ourselves, and as we commit to keep learning and
growing, we have the mindset of a winner. Right
now, the pieces are coming together, and we are
able to get a glimpse of the beautiful masterpiece:
the bigger picture being unfolded.

Am I good enough to be great?
Why settle for average, when you can be great? We
are all born with the ability to be great, yet most
of us realize less than ten percent of our potential,

while only a few rise to extraordinary heights, to become legends in their own right. If we are willing to move to the next level, then the path to greatness begins with one question: "How good do you want to be?" If you want to be the best, then you must be determined to be one of the few people willing to go the extra mile.

Once we understand that our number one resource is our **time,** and our number one asset is our **mind**, we will use them wisely to accomplish our goals. Too many of us are too busy just making a living, and not making a life! Maybe you have questioned your ability to achieve your goal based on the lies you have been told by those around you: that you 'don't have what it takes' or 'you will never make it.'

Right now, you have the power to choose what you want to believe about yourself and stop seeing stability in being average. Don't stop now; go all the way to greatness, by designing the life you want to live. You can make a difference, so use every minute to move forward in the direction of your dreams and don't get caught up in the routine of mediocrity.

> "Greatness stands out, where average fits in. *Be not afraid of greatness. Some are born great; some achieve greatness and others have greatness thrust upon them."*
>
> ~ Shakespeare

The fruits of your labour are manifesting and life looks good 'on the outside', but are you truly satisfied? Surprisingly, this is the stage where many choose to self-assess where they are, in order to find their path to a more comfortable space of self-growth, and this is where their journey to greatness takes on new meaning. Now the main focus at this stage is not about the outcome, but on our journey to find real meaning. It allows us to redefine success on our own terms and prompt us to ask life-changing questions, so we can quickly figure out if we are heading in the right direction.

What if the ladder of success we are climbing up is leaning against the wrong wall? Well, according to Stephen Covey, it will only take us to the wrong place faster. Most of us don't give adequate thought to the path we are on, until we reach the "*If I could live my life over again*" stage of life, but we have the power of choice to turn the page and rewrite a new script right now.

Engaging in constant reflection enables us to track our journey and live purposefully. Our state is crucial because our mind is what separates the average from the great, and as we bring it in alignment, nothing can stop us: not our fears, not our circumstances and not even nature itself.

> *You may have the right calling, right purpose and right gifting, but if you have the wrong perception, your dream will fail in the place of its assignment.*

The Subjectivity of the State of Nature

The state from which you operate, will determine your fate.

The path of the tree is already predetermined by the sower of the seed. No matter how great or strong that tree is, it has no control over its immediate outcome or the circumstances it will be exposed to, because it is planted in one place and cannot move. It is subject to the state of nature, which, in this context, is defined as any outcome over which the decision maker has no control. Research reveals that there are two basic state of nature: favorable and unfavorable or good or bad luck. We don't have to depend on money, luck or life's circumstances to be the determining factor as to how we set our goals or which path we choose (See Ecclesiastes 11:5). The state of nature is subject to God, and He is the One in control.

> **Times and circumstances; the powers of nature and their results are all in the hand of God.**

We have a choice in the hundreds of possible outcomes that daily affect our lives. Many people allow their state, whether their circumstances are favorable or not, to determine their outcome, but that belief is only in their head. We have the choice of deciding what kind of life we will live, and what type of person we want to be.

We are not just a result of how our parents treated us or a product of our environment. We are a result of the choices we make every day. Not all of us were born in ideal situations, but we refused to be defined by them, and choose instead to see the possibilities and contingencies available to us. The truth is, we don't have to conform to what life throws our way, so stop blaming the universe or bad luck for how your life turns out, because you have the final say. Now is the time to take back the controls and cast aside every excuse, as we prepare ourselves to take our life to the next level and get onto the path of greatness.

The genesis of all greatness is a state of mind and quality of heart.

What's the *Shift Required* to change your life's Trajectory?

Your worst enemy is really in your head. Your outcome is dependent on your perspective: the zone from which you choose to operate.

Your trajectory is simply your path in life or the zone in which you operate. If you want to alter your destination or your outcome, change the trajectory of your life. Studies suggests that when we try to make sudden adjustment to our lives without adjusting our mindset, we will revert to what Mother Nature programmed us to do: take the easy route. This path, also known as the path of least resistance, describes the behavior of most species in the biosphere, and is evidenced by rivers, electricity and even google maps, which moves through the easiest route in order to save energy.

Human nature is no different: following the easy path can become a habit that guides our everyday lives. What is required is for us to make a mental shift to push us off nature's path and unto a pathway of purpose. In the same way engineers can change the path of a river by changing the structure of the terrain so the river flows where they want it to go, we too can shift our perspective and change the trajectory of our lives, to create the results we want to achieve.

The truth is, we see the world as we are. Your belief system: how you see yourself and the world, form your inner rules that affects your daily outcome. Now we understand why great achievers are determined to cultivate beliefs that enhance their success, while average people have beliefs that keep them playing small. If you don't take time to understand your innate programming that rules your behavior, you will one day end up in a personal and professional dead end.

If you want to make a change, you first need to address your own internal zones of limitations created by your brain, keeping you on the path of least resistance, based on its automatic programming. We are wired to be lazy, so for this reason, we make decisions based on what is easiest, creating dams and blockages for ourselves by our limited belief system. When we improve our mental pictures, we improve our lives, because these mindsets: these assumptions, which reinforces our preconceived notions about ourselves and our world, are mental barriers that holds us hostage.

When we see differently, we behave differently.

Get out of your Comfort Zone: Get on a Growth Trajectory

Only against resistance in our lives can we grow and move forward.

When you choose greatness, you choose a road less traveled; a road that will test your determination to create something extraordinary. You will never rise to greatness, if you continue to tolerate your propensity to be average. It is a growth trajectory, which includes shedding old layers of yourself that are no longer serving you in order for you to operate from a different zone and begin to own your own path.

The great philosopher Socrates states that the unexamined life is not worth living. There are many dimensions of our lives where we need to examine and throw ourselves into new things in order to learn, thereby, empowering us to confront our comfort zone, move out and live the life of our dreams. Real growth and personal development encompass moving out of your limited zone, getting off the regular road you have become accustomed to, getting unto new paths and unto a trajectory where you are challenged and stretched.

> **The comfort zone is not just about comfort, but it is a lazy zone; the *just getting by* zone; the *cowardice* zone; the *conformist* zone; the *average* zone or the *safety* zone.**

The route within is where true growth occurs. Bottomline, real success is less about results and more about a mindset and behavior, in order to achieve your desired life. There is only one common denominator when we read the autobiographies of great achievers in any field, and that is: success comes from the inside out. External greatness is derived from an internal source; it is a state of mind, not only a goal to achieve. Truth is, your outer world reflects your inner world, and it is only when you elevate your mind by moving from being externally directed, to being more internally directed, can you elevate yourself.

Success versus Greatness

What does success or greatness look like for you? Although the idea of greatness or success is probably as old as time, people still struggle to understand it. You will only be successful by going after what you want, instead of being confined to a life you have stumbled into. Therefore, getting out of your comfort zone starts by getting out of your head (*what others want for you*), and focusing on what is in your heart *(what you want for yourself)*.

> **Success, to some, is an outcome, but greatness is a journey.**
> **Success, based on your interpretation, is earned, but greatness is bestowed.**
> **Greatness is how your everyone around you defines your success.**
> **~ Neil Ducoff**

The greatest thing about the flow of our lives is that it is always trying to push us forward. That means, you stop merely complying with others' expectations and conforming to the current culture. Success is a decision, and every great achiever makes a decision about the future they want to create. It is never too late to change your lane or start all over again. You must know that you have something within you, and that is greatness. Do not allow your head to talk you out of what your heart wants you to do. Even if your circumstances are unfavorable, you can choose to operate from a favorable state of mind, which is your moment-to-moment experience, generated by your thinking, and expressed by your feelings.

Most of us are confined to a life of mediocrity because we can't bother to make a determined effort to pursue what our heart yearns for, so we live like cowards, afraid to move out of our zone of limitations. Many times, we live according to others' expectations of us or we stay stuck in a particular zone, like in a career we have been in because we feel we are already too far climbing the ladder to make a change or in a dead-end relationship that is not going anywhere, but you would rather stay in it and be miserable, than start over again. The overall thrust of your life is like the power of the river's current, surging to get the results you truly want, and when you make the appropriate changes by thinking at a higher level, the path you own for yourself cannot lead anywhere, except in the direction you want to go.

Measure success on your own terms. The real meaning is the meaning you give it.

Visualize yourself as the very best in whatever you do continually. Take steps to pursue your dreams and take your life to the next level.

Dig Deeper

Summary: Grow into your Greatness

TRUTH Do not settle for average, when you can be great. Choose to operate from the right zone, by having the right perspective. Go all the way and do not give into circumstances and excuses; you have a choice in your outcome, so choose wisely.

For Further Research

- Greatness is not an exclusive concept; it is within our reach.
- Understand the impact of how our brain is wired or programmed.
- Importance of being your authentic self and reflecting your light.
- Lessons from Scripture about perspective.
- Identifying your comfort zone and move out of it.
- It is never too late to change your path or change your career.

Related Topics

- Fixed mindset versus growth mindset.
- We see things and people as we are.
- Look at the attitude, mindset, and habits of great people.
- Study the autobiography of the great people you admire.

Conclusion

Before God blesses you with a plan of action, He will burden you with a problem you have been called to solve.

~ Unknown

As we reflect on our journey, we are grateful for having the courage to start, the discipline to submit to the process, and the faith to implement a plan of action. As the signs of the harvest becomes more evident, we are now fully convinced of what lies ahead, as we tap into what we thought was dormant. Our investment of quality time to strengthen our roots has given us great returns and, right now, we are prepared to step into the light and flourish. Not only do we want to flourish, but we want to live out our full potential and go all the way to greatness.

In the field of psychology, there is an ongoing battle between nature versus nurture, both regarded as powerful influencers on our confidence and ability to succeed. But how do these factors shape you? The theory of the nature versus nurture theory seeks to explain this mystery, by positing that it is either nature or nurture that determines who we really are. Nature suggests that the seed can only be what it is genetically programmed to be, regardless of what it is exposed to. Nurture, on the other hand, posits that the potential within each seed is unlocked, once the specific conditions for germination is met. The reality of creation makes it evident that it is both nature and nurture that exposes our real worth.

You don't have to let the first chapter of your life determine the rest of your life. There are no limits out here; only those we impose on ourselves. Once we dream, believe and take action, the world is our oasis. Start now to create the life of your dreams. Start small, dream big and don't ever give up. There is a great deposit in you, and many things you can do, but there is only one thing you have the ability to bring mastery and greatness to, and it is time to pursue it, right now.

The only way that we can live, is if we grow. The only way that we can grow, is if we change. The only way that we can change, is if we learn. The only way we can learn, is if we are exposed. And the only way that we can become exposed, is if we throw ourselves out into the open. Do it. Throw yourself into the open.

~ C. JoyBell C.